Memories are a
Special Gift.

My Rhymes and Reason
A Collection of Poems and Memories Never to be Forgotten

By Lynda Holmes-Kelly

Illustrations by Alan Jones

First published in 2016
Lynda Holmes-Kelly

ISBN-13: 978-1537024943

My Rhymes and Reason
A Collection of Poems and Memories Never to be Forgotten

By Lynda Holmes-Kelly

Illustrations by Alan Jones

CONTENTS

DEDICATION

I would like to dedicate this collection to Raymond Henry Kelly, my dad who was my guiding light and many an inspiration for my thoughts. Also to my absent but very loved brother, Allen and one of our surviving few. Thirdly, my husband, Don who continues to encourage me to live outside my shell.

FOREWORD

Thank you for showing interest in my collection, inspired very often when my chips were down a little. That said, I wrote some of my first poems whilst lying on a sunny, sandy beach in the Bahamas.

I have written these works over the last 25 years and one is titled "Memories are a Special Gift". For anyone to lose the ability to recall all of life's loves, highs and lows is most tragic. Therefore, I have dedicated much of the funds raised by the proceeds of sales to The Alzheimer's Society and wish everyone good health.

This was an occasion where watching a simple TV programme instigated a verse or two.

Goggle Box Blubs

I've just watched a programme
That's made me shed a tear
No horrors or the creepies
That would fill me full of fear
Just some simple entertainment
That makes you value what you have
Not in goodies or materials
But a simple smile or laugh.

When will we truly value
What's most important in life so short
Can we forget about the trinkets
To concentrate on what we ought
That the life that we have been given
Is so fragile and much abused
But would we reconsider
If the outcome could be mused.

If it was our destiny to benefit
From being mortally aware
Would we change our lives significantly
Of our demise, do we truly care
Would we choose to reconsider
And bank more time to just enjoy
Or depend on perpetuity
And continue to toy.

2013

Dad was my best friend and I adored him. He was a very gifted pianist and could also play the accordian. I was brought up on parties that seemed to be weekly and if the piano was not playing in our home for the sing-songs, then the accordian was lovingly taken to the host venue. Losing him was such a heart-breaking time but I felt fortunate to have many dreams about him after he passed away and in one dream actually had a physical hug. Somehow, since Mum has joined him, he doesn't visit so often in my dreams but I know that they are having fun and the party goes on. Often when travelling abroad, I sense their presence close by and am happy that they have decided to come along on the journey.

A Special Dad

Mine was so special
"So was mine", I hear you say,
But we can cherish that bond
Born on our own Birth Day.

A Dad and his Daughter
Has a rapport like no other,
Simply rare and unique
Even from that of a Brother.

He cajoled as he tutored
Loved and cared from the heart,
Those feelings will remain
Even though we are apart.

His smile bore a twinkle
Now found in the stars,
Remembering a laugh rich and warm
That would melt chocolate bars.

His legacy of love
He has so richly endowed,
Leaves the Daughter, I am
Of her Dad, ever so proud.

28th May 2009

Written when feeling a little unappreciated as a wife and something that occurs in all relationships whether male or female. I am pleased to say this was just a moment in time.

Jag the Nag

My wife is like my car
Sort of classy, sometimes sleek
I love my Jaguar.

I drive her hard and very fast
She handles well but the tyres and brakes
Don't always last.

A few dents here, a few bumps there
Throw a few quid in and soon she'll be back
To loving care.

My wife is like my Jag
Generally reliable
Sometimes a nag.

She's a fair runner, no need to spoil
Why has she seized??
Shoot - I forgot the oil!

> *Apart from a few rhyming ditties, this was the first poem I can recall writing. This was written during my time abroad in the Bahamas (Jan88-July90) with my first husband and basically the first time I had been far away from Mum and Dad at Christmas. I do remember feeling quite homesick although having a fantastic time in a fabulous exotic location. I wrote a small collection of poems for the family and remember feeling quite embarrassed to tell anyone about them including my husband. I eventually confided in some girlfriends and they encouraged me to send them home to the family as my gift that year and that was the start of my Rhymes and Reason.*

Bahamian Blues

Xmas upon us soon will be
As I sit here beside the sea
I think of family far away
And wonder if I'll see the day
That they might join me on the sand
Of this small and distant sunny land.

On Xmas day we all could sit
Upon the beach and eat a bit
Of turkey leg and Xmas pud
It would do us all the world of good
To be together for a while
We wouldn't even need a pile
Of money for all our wishes
(I'd even have help to do the dishes).

No, money really could not buy
What I would wish and I will tell you why
Love knows not of distance and miles
And brings us more than cheery smiles
My family's love means more to me
Knowing it's with me whereever I be
And I to them do send my own
To Barney – love in a marrow bone!
Regardless of distance, always together
Bound by love forever and ever.

November 1988

One of the first collection of family poems. We had sadly lost Auntie Doris some years earlier but my memories of those walks to Central Park are still very vivid. Auntie Doris was a tall, elegant lady and in walking beside her I did feel "grand".

Central Park

Auntie Doris took my hand
It felt so grand
As she walked me to the park.

She would sit and stay
While I would play
Until my heart's content.

And if by luck
A tiny duck
Would come and eat some bread.

I'd be so gay
For the rest of the day
Sorry for it to end.

And then back home
After the park we'd roam
For biscuits and some tea.

I'd hear the tick tock
Of the grand old clock
And be happy as can be.

I would cherish
And dearly wish
We could go again one day.

November 1988

Goodbye

Life deals us many bitter blows
Why we should suffer our Lord only knows
But he also gives love
From his heaven above
And if our faith doesn't die
We can more understand why
That all emotions through our life must be felt
From the sad and the happy times, we are dealt
To lose a loved one is a tragic event
But your memories together, from heaven are sent.

24 February 1989

Feeling very sad for a friend back home in the UK whilst I was abroad and not being close enough to share a hug.

Inspired by someone moaning about not being "happy".

Chimes of Time

Pure happiness
Is simply a moment in time,
Measured in life's body clock
As an intermittent chime.

With the tick of a year
And the tock of a life,
Look for contentment
Strike of the strife.

Enjoy every minute,
Take the time to destress.
Savour that moment
…Pure happiness.

 Written for someone very close
who follows a family trait.

Bothered

I think it's in the family
In fact, I'm pretty sure,
And to this day, I do believe
There is no certain cure.

I suppose it is an illness
That rarely goes away,
For some it does cause trouble
Each and every day.

It could be called a habit
That truly is a curse,
And I know of one person
Who is bothered so much worse.

He can be heard to moan and groan
Be desperate for some rest,
It's hard to say whether him or it
Is the awful pest.

Because if the problem was not there
He'd do it all the same,
What is this infliction?
WORRY is its name.

June 1989

For someone who did become stronger

Hopelessness is not Forever

Although at times it might appear
That no-one cares or has time to hear
About your troubles and your worries
And the pain you feel will never ease.

Your present action we cannot condone
But ask you to remember you are not alone
That life is traumatic for all but a few
And the emotions you feel are not confined to just you.

Remember your family love you whatever
But cannot promise happiness forever
You will feel better before very long
Just think of your family and you will be strong.

December 1988

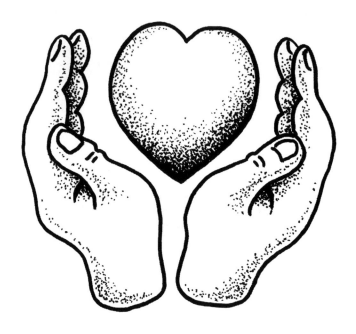

Many of my poems have been written on a whim and literally flow off the pen and this was one of those. I didn't realise that this was actually referring to my own marriage at the time but reading back, my sub-conscious was obviously more aware of problems in my first marriage.

Talk to Me

We sometimes find it hard to say
Exactly what we feel
But written words are the perfect way
To help us to reveal.

What burdens prey on our mind
Or worries ache the heart
But we should really try to find
An alternative to growing apart.

So when it is difficult to converse
Remember this message to you
It need not be returned in verse
I'd be happy with "I love you".

June 1989

" To my half-brother, Allen whom I
adore to this day. He is my big brother
being 10 years older and I vividly
remember, as a little girl, him going
away to boarding school and being so
excited when he returned home, then so
sad when he had to leave again. Even
today we live too many miles apart
from each other but our sibling love
has not diminished.

Naughty Auty

There is one I've loved throughout the years
Although many spent apart,
I loved him then and more so now
From the bottom of my heart.

Separated by circumstances
In different worlds we grew,
Brought together for short vacations
Which were very far and few.

But this past year
Has changed things around,
And a new understanding
Of each other we've found.

We've lived through many dramas
Sharing troubles, fun and even our Mum,
You know who you are
From your own "Smelly Bum"!

November 1988

> Sunday mornings were regularly spent at Guinea Gap baths with Dad followed by a visit to see Auntie Nora and Uncle Tom who lived close to the swimming baths. My cousin, Derek, was usually still in bed having been out the night before with his friends and I was his untimely wakeup call! He was famed for his smelly socks and they were often used in punishment much to everyone's hilarity.

Suffocation by Sock!

He'd lie in bed each Sunday morn
Recovering from drink, tired and worn.
I'd jump on his bed and wake him with glee
'Cos like a brother was Derek, to me.

Effects of hangovers I did not know,
But for the sake of his head I just had to go.
Into the corner covered by a blanket or two
Here comes the smelly sock …OH NO…POOH!!

November 1988

One of my favourite quotes is, "Whoever says money doesn't buy you happiness, doesn't know where to shop"! I love this quote for the fun factor but in truth we often strive for the wrong things in life to give us true peace and contentment.

Richness of Life

Neither money you lust
Or power will entrust,
You'll be happy for
The rest of your life.

What use is such wealth
If you haven't got health?
As your days will bring
Nothing but strife.

Enjoy while you can
For there is surely no man
That at sometime
Endures no ills.

There is nothing as worse
When your body is the curse,
And you are endlessly
Living on pills.

The moral of this prose
From one who knows,
Is that your health
is the ultimate wealth.

March 1990

Remembering my special Dad

Loving Lectures

In a very pensive moment
When the drink does take a hold,
I think of you Dad and remember
All the things that I was told.

I wish I was a little girl
And could sit upon your knee,
I would treasure all the lectures
That you could give to me.

WEDDING DAY

"For my Goddaughter, Laura, on her wedding day and a very proud moment.

To the Blushing Bride

From the long gangly legs
To tresses of glorious curl,
We've watched you transform
From baby to girl.

And what a pleasure
That journey has been,
No terrible tantrums
Or troublesome teen.

We've watched in wonder
As you have built on your life,
To now finding the groom
To make you his wife.

But oh how the years
Have quickly faded away,
To see you standing before us
On this, your wedding day.

Both inside and out
The most beautiful bride,
Who embarks on a future
And fills us with pride.

You are about to start a new album
Of memories and dreams.
May they fill many happy pages
Of love that fills the reams.

On this special day
Our wish for Laura and John,
A cherished future, with love
From Auntie Lynda and Don.

October 2010

I was very young when Nan passed away but she had such a wonderful sense of humour and I recall feeling very safe and loved in her company. This memory is very vivid to me as is another one when visiting Nan – I was standing on the front door step waiting for Auntie Nora to arrive. When I saw her coming up the road I called to her excitedly but she pretended that she didn't know me, as a joke. However, I was so upset I started crying and she was distraught that she had upset me and gave me so many hugs and kisses until I started laughing again.

Merton Road

In that front room of Merton Road
I remember Nan, so dear.
Although so ill she held me close
And I felt love warm and near.

She loved to laugh and have such fun
And any chance to joke,
And to this day I can recall
The very words she spoke.

"Here comes your Auntie Nora,"
Seen from the window by Mother.
"Quickly you must hide
And snuggle here under the cover."

November 1988

This was for one of my
Goddaughters, Alex, inspired
by her Christening.

Christening Day

A little bundle born with love
And cherished by our Lord above.
We hope and pray that she may be
Caring, contented and of course, healthy.

Beauty she has already found
And endless admirers through her life will abound.
Together with nature sunny and sweet
Will certainly sweep many off their feet.

Her parents she has made the happiest,
With their endless love, she will be blessed.
Alex, we all dearly wish for you
That all your dreams in life come true.

June 1989

Late at night staying over at a friend's house, alone and missing my husband (my pearl), Don. My star sign is Cancer and I do occasionally want to hide in my shell, however Don has encouraged me to come out of my shell and inspired me to do so much more with my life and given me the confidence I was lacking in my earlier years. I do, however, still enjoy the odd night on the "rocks" with good friends.

One Night on the Rocks

I was a little crab
and lived inside my shell,
'Cos the world outside was scary
And didn't always treat me well.

Some people found me fascinating
And others found me scary,
Children would like to chase me
And as for those who'd cook me, I was more than wary!

I took to finding shelter
From the hurtful taunts and mocks,
Spending the days on the seaweed
And the nights on the rocks.

On a sideways walk on the beach one day,
I met a very strange fishy called "jell",
Who told me that despite all of life's stings,
It can also treat you well.

I took heed of his words
And went about life with more 'boister',
Then found my pearl of a life mate,
Who showed me that the world is my oyster.

August 2012

My first audience at a Bahamian pool team league match, found me chuckling when instead of referring to the balls as "spots" or "stripes" the Bahamians called them "big balls" and "little balls". After the first ball went down and the referee announced that John had "big balls" you can imagine the hilarity all around, together with a smug-looking John!!!

Right on Cue

He's ready to break
And looks quite cool,
But will he win
His game of pool.

The white ball hits the pack
Like a rocket.
But which one will fall
Down into the pocket?

Over the crowd
anticipation falls,
As they wait to find out
Who has big or small balls.

Big balls it is
but I already knew.
I had that sussed out,
When he chalked up his cue.

Bahamian pool team 1987/1990

*Staying with friends in their villa in Gremacho,
Portugal. Sitting quietly in the sunshine,
nursing a "slight" hangover (from one of those
nights on the rocks) and waiting for everyone
else to wake and journey into the sunshine and
another glorious day.*

A Leap into Paradise

Trickling waters in the pool of azure blue,
Floating blossoms that the wind once blew.
An array of greens in this tranquil spot
Made perfect by the sun gleaming and hot.

Splashes of purples, pinks and fronds of blue,
Adorn the gardens of the multi-coloured hue.
An array of birds in melodic song
Make this indulgence in nature far from wrong.

A splash and splish of a leaping frog
To take a dip leaves us agog.
Will he drown or be doomed to filter fatality?
No he hops out refreshed, to our hilarity.

With oranges, lemons and olives in sight
To sit here and wonder is this glorious day's plight.
What sunbed, what factor, what drink do I choose?
Just go with the flow, there is nothing to lose!

July 2014

*We were
introduced
to this hotel
in Spain by
very close friends and have been
fortunate to have several trips
here with them during the past
few years. This poem remembers
a significant phone call received,
at a previous visit, bringing
fantastic news and an end to a
torturous time for our friends. It
prompted the booking of another
trip for a birthday celebration.*

El Oceano

Your birthday celebration
In this haven in the sun,
Brings special friends together
In life's lottery of fun.

This bolt hole, El Oceano
Has certainly made its mark.
For laughter, fun and life's finery
Chasing past torments in the dark.

But now we are here
In the "pink" element of bliss.
It does make you wonder
How can it get any better than this?

17th August, 2014

> *I became quite homesick on the lead up to my first Christmas living abroad. I was thinking of all the family past and present and not having written any poetry in the past I still don't know where these came from. I still have very vivid memories of Pop and his visits after Nan passed away. I didn't like Jelly Babies in those days, but they are now one of my favourites!*

Sweet Memories

My dear old Pop
I can recall
From when I was only
very small.

Each visit he made
He brought me treats
Not knowing I cared not
for those jellied sweets.

He'd twiddle his thumbs
Whilst sitting there
In that big old
Fireside chair.

Too young to realise
On the day that he died
I later missed visits
And then that I cried.

One day in particular
I was unhappy and glum.
"Please can I have
Some Jelly Babies, Mum?"

Written in Bahamas 1988

Mum married for the third time at 71 to her "toyboy" of 61, Dave. Dave is a lovely man and loved and looked after Mum for the short few years they were together before she passed away. This poem was written on the morning of the wedding sitting in a cafe and scribbled on a paper napkin as the words flowed. I had bought a Wedding Day card but simply could not think of anything suitable to write in it. I was very happy for Mum but also a little sad, remembering Dad. The whole poem literally came to me in an instant and still brings a tear to my eye.

A Special Gift

Memories are a special gift
Likened to an album of the mind,
Where we store life's happy moments
And maybe some that weren't so kind.

Yet another special ability
Is the ability to love,
Whether you are a young love-struck teenager
Or even 60 or above.

A love that's found in later years
Doesn't erase any memories of the past,
It merely opens up new pages
Of a memento built to last.

So if you are lucky to find another
To share and love within your life,
What better declaration
Than, "I pronounce you, Man and Wife."

For Mum and Dave 1996

Before I knew my "ex" was going to be my "ex"!

Ring of Truth

Did he lose his wedding ring?
I've wondered in the past.
Or did he try to remove it
Too pretty damn fast?

In a bar with girls, it seems
Pretty strange to me.
Or was it simply to deny
His own matrimony.

Bahamas April 1989

> I think everyone has one of these moments and nothing beats a smile; it's free and infectious.

Reflections

There are times in our life
When nothing goes right,
And day to day living
Is one endless strife.

But life has its good times
And not always bad,
When memories recalled
Are far happier, than sad.

So when in our hearts
We feel nothing but pain,
It's to those good times
We must look again.

At past laughter and fun
And there, linger a while.
Then look in the mirror
And there see a smile.

1990

Forster Frolics

14 years young when I first met the family
22 when I shared the Forster name.
Some 44 years on and many special memories
That are not always recalled the same.

But to me, Bill and Jean at the heart and core
Of this family of fun,
Welcomed me in
When I first met their son.

With two older brothers
Who ribbed and cajoled,
And a blond, blue-eyed little sister
Who didn't always do as she was told!

Parties were many with
Jean's roast dinners for all.
The girls did the dishes
Washing and drying from wall to wall.

Dirty plates, clean plates
And plates tucked away deep.
All passed through the convoy
Before we all fell in a heap.

Rugby pitch sidelines
With my future In-Law Mam,
Introduced me to the intoxication
Of Baby and Brandy-sham!

Charades was a family favourite
And Geoff's "turtle's progress" a beholden scene.
Was that the first time
We gave the name to "Jissy Pean"?

Balking tackwards and
wisting our twerds, so well said
Until Pa was faced
With the duck feather bed!

Even of late, in her illness,
Humour did not go away.
And Ma still made us laugh
With the things that she would say.

So much to recall
Of happiness and fun
We will all so much miss
One very special Mum.

In memory of my "ex" Mum-in-law, Jean, who suffered from dementia and sadly passed away in January 2015. I have been fortunate since my divorce from my first husband to have retained great relationships with all the family and consider myself lucky to have "out-laws" and "in-laws"!

This poem was written
after losing a much
loved sister-in-law.

Dawn

Bravery comes in many ways
From heroic deeds on battle days.
But it is not isolated to the military ground
And in everyday life more commonly found.

When illness brings a family to the lowest of low,
Their love and bonding can still make the sunshine glow.
When the family's core member is the one who's distressed,
And she still holds you all together in her maternal nest.

A very special lady who lived her final days to the full
Leaving memories of her so beautiful,
Now a twinkling star through night to morn
To the glistening dew drops...Dawn.

This poem is what it says and I must thank Jo
Howarth from The Happiness Club for her insights
and tools, which have proved fantastic and helped
me to destress!! I also have to thank her for
encouraging me to attend as the workshop venue was
the fabulous home of Sue Miller, who has brought
this book together and encouraged me to complete
the process. That one day has given me so many
reasons to smile and I am extremely happy that it
was the start of this collection being published.

In Search of Happiness

Driving to a Happiness Workshop
Out in Wrexham, one day,
Had me wondering where "it" was
As I went on my way.

The stress and the pressure of
A frantic and busy life,
Had left me subdued
On the edge of a knife.

But the journey itself
Brought a smile to my face,
The low winter sun
Beamed with beauty and grace.

Quaint villages and the greenery
Glistened in the sunlight,
And each meandering road travelled
Brought its own special delight.

The venue located
And a vision to behold,
The most wonderful cottage and manor house
Where you would love to grow old.

But that memorable driveway
That brought down my defence,
Was seeing the doe-eyed cows
Smiling from over the fence.

The day had started well
And I have to confess,
That a location near Wrexham
Was where I found "Happiness".

January 2016

*For a work colleague on
her wedding day*

Wedding Breakfast

The morning of your wedding
Should be calm and quite serene,
With breakfast in bed; in other words,
Be treated like a queen.

Just make the most of the attention
It won't always be this way,
After the months of preparation
It will prove the shortest day.

Forget about the worries,
Though nerves may take a hold.
Enjoy every single minute,
As every bride is told.

The weather will not matter
You will be happy to be wed,
Even more so later
When you're both snuggled up in bed.

1991

As a little girl I adored Auntie Nora and Uncle Tom and spent a lot of time with them. When I couldn't stay at their's for dinner, I would ask to take some of Auntie Nora's gravy home in a bag. They were members of the Caravan Club and I often went with them. In those days there was no inside toilet and thus "the bucket" for night-time convenience!

The Caravan Club

Thinking back while here I laze,
I remember fun-filled caravan days
With Auntie Nora and Uncle Tom it was such fun,
And cavorting with girls, was cousin Derek, their son.

They took me with them on lots of trips,
Auntie Nora had us rolling with all of her quips
About herself and things around,
And of Uncle Tom, they did abound.

I'm sure he didn't really mind
As nothing was ever meant unkind.
But oh how we laughed without a care,
When he sprayed deodorant on his hair.

When he hit his head, we could have died.
Tried not to laugh – "You Nits," he cried.
But silently he laughed when I just had "to go".
I sat on the bucket whilst holding his toe.

Yes, I remember those days fondly with glee
And hope they didn't feel burdened with me.
I'm sure they didn't and love me as I
Love them more and more as the years pass by.

Year of '98

Birthdays come around just about every year,
But fly past with quickening speed.
Warnings when young, of life passing you by
Are regarded with little or usually no heed.

Now in my 41st year, I look back a mere twenty
To a garden celebration complete with marquee.
That was certainly "a do" with all drunk but a few,
Provided with love from Mum and Daddy.

Yet another outdoor event remembered by some
Was a certain momentous and fateful barbecue.
When I was drawn into eyes, I didn't realise,
It would lead us to saying "I do".

Yet that day was to be a beginning for me,
Although, unaware of the diversity.
Whisked from the Bahamian shores
To far more exotic shores of a village called New Ferry!

We withstood all the complications
That should have kept us apart.
Thankful that the reasoning heads were overruled
By the more powerful, trusting hearts.

I could not ever now imagine
A more fulfilling and varied life,
Than the one I am currently living
As Don's partner, "tart", mate and wife.

Here I will cheat and adapt a few lines,
That a celebrated poet once wrote.
Which I feel do suitably express
My feelings, so therefore I quote:

"You have me locked in your fortress
From which I never want to depart,
Forever to be held in the dungeon
Of the round tower of your heart.

"There I will stay forever
Forever and a day,
Until the walls shall crumble in old age
Leaving memories of our days making hay!"

So for yesterday, today and tomorrow
In front of family, friends of old and of new,
I would like to state categorically,
Don, I am deeply in love with you.

6th July 1998

*A birthday celebration
some 18 years ago and
I can happily say that
this poem could have
been written yesterday. Yes, we have
journeyed the rollercoaster of life
together, some enjoyable and others
not so. I have no doubt there are
more adventures in the future for
us but it is a future together and we
look forward to the journey.*

Written on a plane listening to Rhapsody in Blue which was one of Dad's signature tunes, having trained classically as a young man. When I was old enough to read a little music I would turn the pages of the music sheets for this particular piece. I remember these occasions so well and that he had clipped some pages together to abbreviate to the main piano refrains.

Blue for You

Remembering the tinkling of the ivories
Filling our home with delight,
From boogie woogie to syncopation
Or a classical Gershwin night.

I wish I had had the dedication
To learn the talent you wished to share,
I dabbled, but now regret
I ignored the foresight to care.

What fun. What parties!
You were the best musical host
Or invited with accordian, the guest
Whom all would like the most.

I was brought up on fun and laughter,
With your music in my ears.
Leaving my memories of youth
Such very special years.

Dad
We all loved you.
Without your own special rhapsody,
I still feel blue.

27th April 2016

I couldn't leave out a verse or two about Tilly-Mint, our current dog who arrived on Christmas Eve 2013 as a most wonderful gift from very close friends. She is our second Samoyed having adopted our first boy, Symba, at 10 years old. Symba was nearly 15 when he died and such a wonderful character, however Tilly is certainly proving to be an amazing personality in her own right and very easy to love.

Tornado Tilly

A four legged puff ball of fluff,
Arrived one Christmas Eve.
Uncertain of her future
Parted from her brothers she had to leave.

Her snow fox features
And blond eyelashes so cute,
Turned devil incarnate in the wee hours
When she was impossible to mute.

Playtime and freedom
Was the, too early, order of the day.
No cajoling or reprimand
Would allow us to slumber away.

The etiquette of home life
She was not in the know.
And preferred the playground of garden,
Where she could kill all that would grow.

She dug holes in the lawn,
Ripped the branches from trees.
Left a multitude of patches
From her poops and her wees.

We were amazed at the debris
From one so cute and so little.
How she would strip bark from tree branches,
And proceeded to whittle.

My new winter coat
Was stolen from the chair,
Dragged through the garden
To become part of her lair.

Squirrels were bait
To drive her so silly.
Instigating our very own whirlwind
Called "Tornado Tilly".

Then one day
She simply grew up,
Turning into little Miss Princess
From mischievous pup.

Now she reclines in style
In between doggie pampers and spas.
Chauffeured to work
In Mum or Dad's car.

Yes, she is part of the staff,
On daily salary of chew stick.
Employed to de-stress
With tail wag and dog lick.

Taking staff holidays abroad
Through Eurotunnel and port,
Visited France, Spain and Portugal
Holding her own passport.

But she does her job well,
Never complains of her stint.
Loved by us and her colleagues
Is our own Tilly-Mint.

ACKNOWLEDGEMENTS

I have been encouraged over the years by friends and family to put this collection together. A chance meeting with the lovely Susan Miller from All Words Matter, gave me the encouragement to put the plan into action. I told her of my idea of having specific illustrations and my search for someone who could help me with this. Sue introduced me to the very talented illustrator, Alan Jones who simply "got it" and I am sure you will agree that his work enhances my ramblings. Without both Susan and Alan my book would still be an idea in progress and I thank them for all their input and support in bringing this together. I would also like to thank Ellen Parzer for her design and creativity. Finally, to all my friends and family who have inspired my writing whether you knew it or not!

ABOUT THE AUTHOR

Lynda was born in Wallasey on the Wirral, just across the River Mersey from Liverpool in 1957. She was the only child of Ray and Agnes but has an older half-brother Allen, whom she adores to this day. Allen lives in America but they get together as often as they possibly can.

Lynda had a very happy childhood and began her career in banking following in the footsteps of her father in 1974 but left when a career opportunity arose for her first husband, to live in the Bahamas for 3 years in 1987-1990.

It was during this period that her first poems and recollections were made whilst sitting in glorious surroundings but with a feeling of being homesick for her parents and family, whom she had always been very close to and missing her first Christmas with them all.

Circumstances brought her home to the UK in 1990 and in that year she met Don. They subsequently married in 1995 and Lynda was fortunate to also gain a fantastic step-son Darren who has always been not just a son but a great friend to her as well. Don and Lynda have a successful business together and continue to build on that, having in recent years franchised their company, which is growing steadily.

Over the past 25 years they have loved their adopted dogs - first being Sam a short haired German Shepherd followed by another Sam, a long-haired German Shepherd. Then along came the lovely Symba a 10 year old Samoyed (yet another "Sam") who amazingly lived a puppyish life until he was 15.

Tilly-Mint, aka Tornado Tilly, is currently in residence and their fourth "Sam" arriving as a four-month-old Samoyed puppy as a gift from very close friends.

Lynda and Don love to travel together and escape at every opportunity possible and Tilly-Mint has her own passport too!

Twitter: @LynHolmesKelly
Facebook: facebook.com/LynHolmesKelly

Made in the USA
Charleston, SC
05 November 2016